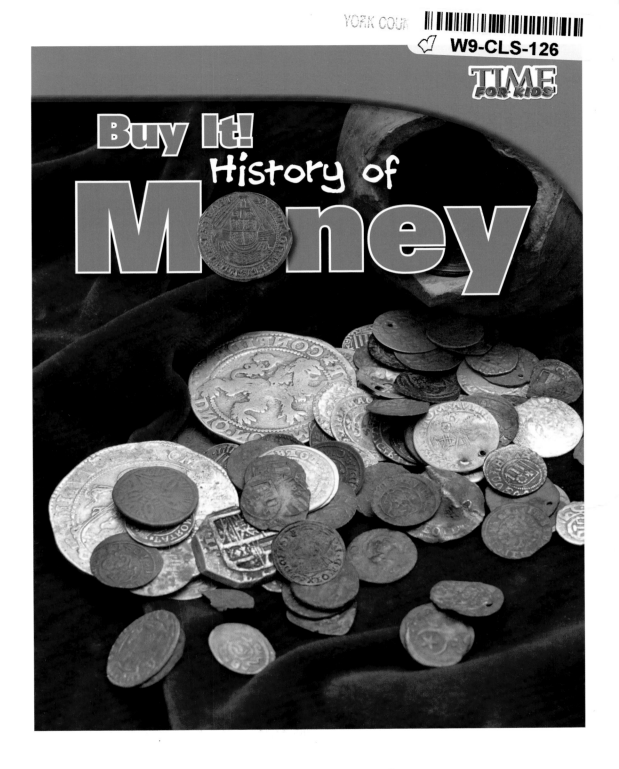

Buy It!
History of
Money

TIME
FOR KIDS

Debra J. Housel

Consultant

Timothy Rasinski, Ph.D.
Kent State University

Publishing Credits

Dona Herweck Rice, *Editor-in-Chief*

Robin Erickson, *Production Director*

Lee Aucoin, *Creative Director*

Conni Medina, M.A.Ed., *Editorial Director*

Jamey Acosta, *Editor*

Heidi Kellenberger, *Editor*

Lexa Hoang, *Designer*

Leslie Palmer, *Designer*

Stephanie Reid, *Photo Editor*

Rachelle Cracchiolo, M.S.Ed., *Publisher*

Based on writing from *TIME For Kids*.

TIME For Kids and the *TIME For Kids* logo are registered trademarks of TIME Inc. Used under license.

Teacher Created Materials

5301 Oceanus Drive
Huntington Beach, CA 92649-1030
http://www.tcmpub.com
ISBN 978-1-4333-3681-2
© 2012 Teacher Created Materials, Inc.

Table of Contents

Before There Was Money

Imagine you are a sheep farmer from long ago. You have enough wool to make two blankets. But, you need a shovel for your land. There's no store or catalog. The only way to get a shovel is to visit the toolmaker who lives miles away. Without money, you must trade, or **barter**, what you have to get what you want.

sheep farmer

You walk to the toolmaker's home with the blankets. He looks them over. Then, he says he will trade a shovel for the blankets. You agree. The two of you have made a good trade.

Does this sound like a good system? It's what everyone did long ago to get what they needed. Such bartering is still done in some places of the world. But, there are some problems with bartering. For example, the toolmaker may not have needed blankets. Also, the sheep farmer had to travel miles to get what he wanted.

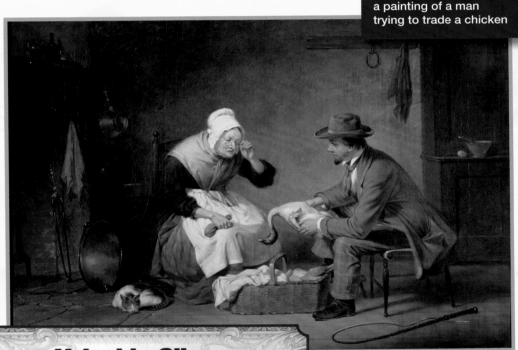

a painting of a man trying to trade a chicken

Valuable Silver

Silver is rare. In 2500 B.C., the people in what is now Iraq stamped the weights of silver bars on the bars themselves. The heavier the bars, the greater their value. The bars could then be used for trade.

The Power of Money

Our world has changed a lot. Most people no longer barter. Everyone uses money to buy the things we need. Did you know that kids in the United States spend more than $15 million of their own money each year? What do you use your money to buy?

The Invention of Money

Over time, people realized that something had to be agreed on to stand for **value**. Value is what something is worth. The first things used as money had values of their own. For example, cows had value because they gave milk. Spices were valuable because they were hard to find and everybody wanted them.

At one time, spices were popular items to trade.

Coins

Slowly people realized the item itself didn't need to be valuable. As long as everyone agreed, such things as feathers, shells, and **wampum** (WOM-puhm) could be used as money. People took these things in **exchange** for work or goods. They knew that others would do the same in exchange for what they wanted. But this system had problems, too. Feathers blew away. Shells broke. People needed something easy to store and carry. As a result, they started making coins.

Wampum is a form of money made of colorful beads cut from shells and woven into belts.

Furs

American Indians used furs as money. Furs were traded for axes, cloth, fishhooks, and other goods.

In 640 B.C., the King of Lydia made the first **standard** coins. They were stamped with a lion's image. Each coin had a set value. This meant that people didn't have to weigh them like the silver bars to decide their value. These coins quickly became popular. Some people secretly changed the value of coins. They cut off the edges and kept the shavings. This meant the coins were not worth as much as people believed. This practice continued until the invention of the coin press in 1660. After that, coins had a regular shape.

Lydia, now Turkey, made the first standard-weight coins out of electrum. Electrum is a natural mixture of gold and silver.

Early Chinese Coins

About 3,000 years ago, the Chinese used tiny bronze tools as their coins. But they did not have standard sizes and weights as the Lydian coins did.

pieces of eight

Pine Tree Shillings

A shilling is a value of money. By law, only the English king could issue shillings for the American colonists. Yet the Massachusetts Bay colonists made pine tree shillings from 1652 to 1682. Every coin was marked 1652. During that year, there was no English king. This made it appear that all the coins were minted while the law wasn't in effect.

Spanish **pieces of eight** were the most common money in the world until 1850. People made change by chopping one of these coins into eight pieces. Each piece was called a **bit**.

Today's coins are an **alloy**, or mixture, of copper and nickel or zinc. First, rollers press the heated metal into thin sheets. Then, a machine punches out blank coins. Finally, the blanks enter a coin press. It **mints** both sides at the same time.

Blank coins are minted at a rate of 600 per minute.

Did You Know?

Today banks collect worn and damaged coins. They send them to be melted down and minted into new coins.

Paper Money

The Chinese started using paper money in A.D. 806. In 1295, the explorer Marco Polo told people in Europe about it. Paper was easier to carry than heavy bags of coins. Yet Europeans did not adopt the idea. They didn't trust that paper money was real money.

ancient Chinese paper money

Gifts to the Dead

In an ancient Chinese tradition, special paper money is burned to send funds to dead relatives.

Banking began with people leaving their coins at a goldsmith's shop.

Gold and Silver Exchange

Until the 1930s, you could exchange paper money for gold or silver coins at banks throughout the world.

During the 1500s, people began leaving coins with a goldsmith for safekeeping. He held them in an **account**. He gave the owner a paper **banknote**. Banknotes were a way to say, "I owe you this amount." They could be used to buy things. The person who held a note could trade it for the coins at the goldsmith's shop. People started using these notes for money.

Today, high-speed presses print the designs for paper money, called *notes*, on big sheets. Machines cut the sheets into stacks of bills. Each month, new bills and coins are sent to banks. The banks put the cash into **circulation**. The money moves from person to person.

Today most nations print their own paper money.

Each nation chooses its own money, called **currency** (KUR-uhn-see). A currency's value is based on how much it can buy. Its value can rise or fall. Around the world, there are different types of currency. But the most widely used currency in the world is the United States dollar.

In 1914, the **Federal Reserve** opened as the central bank of the United States. *Federal Reserve Note* appears at the top of each US bill.

Did You Know?

Banks collect worn bills and send them to the government for shredding. After about 18 months of use, most US dollar bills wear out. Over $400 million dollars in replacement bills are printed daily.

The Exchange Rate

The **exchange rate** shows how one currency compares with another. It changes every day, because a currency's true value is always changing. It changes because of the strength of a country's **economy**. The economy is the system of money, products, and labor in a country. If all of these things are doing well, then a country's economy is strong.

COUNTRY	CURRENCY	WE SELL
UNITED STATES ÉTAS-UNIS		1.1998
EUROPEAN UNION UNION EUROPÉENNE		1.4996
ENGLAND ANGLETERRE		2.1998
JAPAN JAPON		0.0109
SWITZERLAND SUISSE		0.9895
AUSTRALIA		

The exchange rate changes daily.

INTERNATIONAL CURRENCIES

Country	Currency
United States	dollar
Canada	dollar
Ecuador	sucre
United Kingdom	pound
European nations	euro
Israel	shekel
Japan	yen
Kenya	shilling
Mexico	peso
Nicaragua	cordoba
Russia	ruble

Without euros in Europe, it would almost be like people in the United States having to exchange dollars every time they went to another state! The countries in yellow have adopted the euro.

Europe

Where to Use the Euro

These are the 23 countries that have adopted the euro: Andorra, Austria, Belgium, Cyprus, Estonia, Finland, France, Germany, Greece, Ireland, Italy, Kosovo, Luxembourg, Malta, Monaco, Montenegro, the Netherlands, Portugal, San Marino, Slovakia, Slovenia, Spain, and Vatican City.

In January 2002, some European nations switched to the **euro** (YOOR-oh). They stopped using their old currencies. The nations are near one another. When people went from one to the other, they had to exchange their own money for that of the other nation. If they didn't, they couldn't buy things. With more people using the euro, it was easier to do business.

Old Money

What are francs, liras, and drachmas? They are all types of money that do not exist anymore. They used to be the money of France, Italy, and Greece, but now all of those nations use the euro.

Troubles with Money

Every system of trade has its troubles. Money is no different. For example, money is easily stolen and lost. Paper and coins are easier to grab than the earliest bartered items such as cows.

Another problem came about when banks loaned lots of money. People used these same banks to store their savings. If too many people came to collect their savings, the banks did not have enough money on hand to give them because they had loaned out so much. When this happened, the banks **failed**. Some people lost all their money in this way. Now, banks have lending limits so they will not fail.

Paper money usually has a complicated design, special numbers, and tough paper so that it is difficult to counterfeit.

A final problem is that someone somewhere is always trying to copy money. **Forgery** is a crime. So, governments make bills hard to copy. They use fancy patterns and ink made from secret formulas. They print bills on special paper. Even so, some people manage to **counterfeit** (KOUN-ter-fit), or copy, the bills anyway.

The idea of pirate treasure is no myth. Pirates really did steal all the money they could from helpless people.

Pirates

Ships used to carry chests filled with coins. Pirates lay in wait and then attacked ships. Although they look different from the pirates of old, there are still pirates on the seas today. You might even say that bank robbers are pirates on land!

Money Today

Do you have a bank account? It's a good way to store **funds** until you want to spend them. The bank gives you **interest**. Then, the bank lends your money to someone else. The person who borrows it must repay the money plus some interest. That's how the bank makes money.

Most adults put money into a **checking account**. Then, they can write **checks** or use a **debit card** to pay for things, and the money comes out of their accounts.

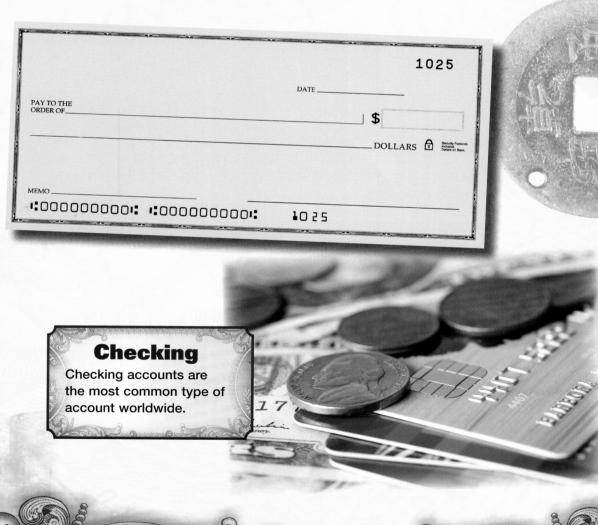

Checking

Checking accounts are the most common type of account worldwide.

Banks today are a safe and secure way to save your money.

Interest

Imagine your sister needs to borrow $1,000 to buy books for college. The bank will give her a loan. The bank makes money by charging a fee. This fee is called interest. Imagine the bank charges $20 interest. That means when she repays the loan, she will owe $1,020.

Kate needs $1,000 to pay for books.

The bank will loan her $1,000.

The bank charges $20 in interest.

Kate owes the bank $1,020.

Debit cards work like electronic checks. When you use a debit card in a store, the money leaves your checking account. It moves to the store's bank account. These cards also work at **automatic teller machines** (**ATMs**). Even when the bank is closed, you can **deposit** or **withdraw** money at an ATM.

Automatic teller machines are called *ATMs.*

Credit cards look like debit cards. But they are very different. With a credit card, you buy things with a promise to pay later. You use the credit card to record your purchase. You will receive a bill each month. You can pay the bill in full or just pay part and carry a **balance**. If you carry a balance, you must pay interest to the credit card company. This means you pay more for things in the end.

Whatever you buy on credit must still be paid for later.

Credit Card Tips

Credit cards can be used around the world. If your credit card is stolen, you don't have to pay for the things you didn't buy. But you also have to be careful with your credit card. Be sure you can pay back what you charge plus interest. And remember to always pay your bills on time.

Many people access their money through online accounts. Banks allow customers to check account balances and conduct business online. Then when the person buys something online, money is sent from the bank account to the business's account. This makes some people think that one day we'll no longer use cash. Funds may simply go from one computer account to another.

More and more people are banking online.

You may be able to earn money by performing chores or helping neighbors. If you have saved a lot of money, it is smart to open a savings account at a bank.

Money Time Line

To see the history of money at a glance, take a look at this time line.

6500 B.C.	The first-known bartering records are written in Egypt.
2500 B.C.	Silver is used as money in Mesopotamia (now southern Iraq).
1800 B.C.	Bronze rings are used as money in northern Europe.
1200 B.C.	Cowrie shells are used as money in China.
750 B.C.	Lumps of electrum are used as money in Lydia (now Turkey).
640 B.C.	The king of Lydia orders standardized gold coins to be made.
500 B.C.	The Chinese make coins in the shape of tiny tools.
400 B.C.	Copper weights are used as money in Russia and Italy.
336 B.C.	The first coins are stamped with a ruler's image (Alexander the Great).
A.D. 806	The Chinese make the first paper money.

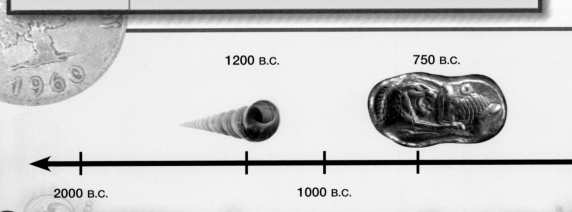

1200 B.C.   750 B.C.

2000 B.C.   1000 B.C.

A.D. **1520**	Handwritten paper banknotes are used in Europe.
A.D. **1609**	The first official bank opens in the Netherlands.
A.D. **1660**	The coin press is invented.
A.D. **1661**	Swedish Stockholm Bank issues the first printed banknote in Europe.
A.D. **1792**	The United States Congress sets the silver dollar as the national currency of the United States.
A.D. **1913**	The United States Congress creates the Federal Reserve and names it the country's central bank.
A.D. **1946**	The World Bank and the International Monetary Fund help worldwide banking.
A.D. **1961**	Computerized banking starts at Chase Manhattan Bank in New York City.
A.D. **1973**	Automatic teller machines are made available for public use.
A.D. **1998**	Online accounts allow the electronic transfer of money.

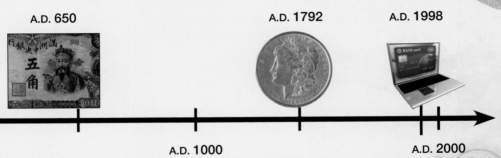

A.D. **650** A.D. **1792** A.D. **1998**

A.D. **1000** A.D. **2000**

Glossary

account—a record of money received or paid out

alloy—a mixture of two or more metals

automatic teller machines (ATMs)—machines that let you deposit or withdraw money from your account even if the bank is closed or you're far away from home

balance—the amount by which one side of an account is greater than the other

banknote—a piece of paper that may be used as money

barter—to trade goods or services for other goods or services

bit—a piece cut from a Spanish dollar known as a *piece of eight*

checking account—a banking account from which a person can write a check or use a debit card

checks—documents, usually pieces of paper, that order money to be paid from one account to another

circulation—moving from person to person (or place to place)

counterfeit—to make a false copy in order to deceive

credit cards—plastic cards with which one can buy things now, promising to pay later

currency—the basic unit of money for a nation

debit card—a plastic card with which a person can move money directly from the person's bank account into someone else's account

deposit—to place for safekeeping

economy—the system of money, products, and labor in a country

euro—a common currency adopted by 23 European nations in 2002

exchange—trade

exchange rate—how one currency compares with another

failed—ran out of money; went bankrupt; stopped operating

Federal Reserve—the central bank of the United States

forgery—the making of fake money

funds—the available supply of money

interest—the money paid to a lender, or money received from a borrower

mints—stamps a design on a piece of metal, usually a coin

pieces of eight—large Spanish coins made of silver

standard—a set number, weight, or value

value—what something is worth

wampum—a form of money made of cut shells

withdraw—to take out

Index

About the Author

Debra Housel worked as a teacher for more than 12 years before becoming a writer. She lives in upstate New York with her husband and three children.